TEDDY BEAR QUOTATIONS

A COLLECTION OF BEAUTIFUL PICTURES AND THE BEST TEDDY QUOTES

— ◆ —

ILLUSTRATED BY
WENDY TRINDER

EXLEY
NEW YORK • WATFORD, UK

"Many a heart learns to love from its first teddy bear."

A.K.

"Cuddly and warm, these calming creatures reassure me in the days when fears fly before reason and the world looms bleak instead of beautiful. The Teddy Bear, all things to all ages . . . symbol that all is right with the world if one only believes."

ANONYMOUS

"I read somewhere the Teddy bear is 'a symbol used by people of all ages to recapture infant security in the face of frightening new situations.' I don't know; I just feel better having him around."

EDWARD McGETTIGAN

"Bears are just about the only toy that can lose just about everything and still maintain their dignity and worth."

SAMANTHA ARMSTRONG

"What is the secret of Teddy bears' instant success and enduring popularity? Very simply, they are irresistible — even those who've had their fur loved off or their paws injured."

PEGGY BIALOSKY AND ALAN BIALOSKY

"A bear remains a bear — even when most of him has fallen off or worn away."

CHARLOTTE GRAY

"The growth of sophisticated electronics has been paralleled by an extraordinary expansion in the soft toy industry. Bears and bunnies and puppy dogs, once confined to the nursery, are now preferred as lover's gifts. White teddy bears in top hats and veils invade the marriage bed. It is difficult to evade the burgeoning of saucer-eyed Woodland Folk on greetings cards for almost every occasion. Faced by the devastating forces which modern science has unleashed, mankind seems to be turning for comfort to a vast amorphous Teddy Bear."

PAM BROWN

"When a child loves you for a long, long time, not just to play with, but REALLY loves you, then you become Real. Generally, by the time you are Real, most of your hair has been loved off, and you get loose in the joints and very shabby. But these things don't matter at all, because once you are Real, you can't be ugly — except to people who don't understand."

MARGERY WILLIAMS

— ♦ —

"It takes a lot of loving to turn a shop bear
into a friend."

PAM BROWN

"My granddaughter was given several bears of
various shapes and sizes. Only one became a
Bear, to be taken everywhere and turned to in
every emergency. That was White Teddy.
He was blue."

PAM BROWN

"The world is divided into two nations. Those with teddy bears, those without. Each thinks the other odd."

JENNY DE VRIES

"I think they're the cutest, dearest, best-behaved little visitors we've ever entertained. I draw the line at their going to church, though."

MRS. HARRY HASTINGS

"As a cleaner I have a set standard by which I judge a new employer. I consider them civilized if there is a cat on the sofa and a bear on the bed."

PAM BROWN

"Here is Edward Bear, coming downstairs now, bump, bump, bump, on the back of his head, behind Christopher Robin. It is, as far as he knows, the only way of coming downstairs, but sometimes he feels that there really is another way, if only he could stop bumping for a moment and think of it. And then he feels that perhaps there isn't. Anyhow, here he is at the bottom, and ready to be introduced to you, Winnie-the-Pooh."

A. A. MILNE
from "Winnie-the-Pooh" —

"A bear grows more alive with age. No one with one ounce of sensitivity could ever consign a bear to the dustbin."

JOHNNIE HAGUE

— ♦ —

"How many children, do you suppose, have carried a lifelong resentment of parents responsible for the surreptitious removal of their Teddy bears?"

JOHN ZIFF

"It is impossible to put the most dilapidated bear in the bin. Honorable burial is the *only* way."

P. MACDONALD

"I regret burning my old love letters, giving away my teenage records and leaving to travel light. But it's Ted I miss most of all."

WENDY FULLER

"There's no bear like an old bear."

SAMANTHA ARMSTRONG

"At sales every other toy looks simply worn, dilapidated, grubby. A bear looks lost and abandoned and desperately in need of a loving home."

HELEN THOMSON

"Bears are like cats — they arrive disguised as nonentities. Only time will reveal just who they really are."

JOHNNIE HAGUE

"As a Speech Therapist, I scored over anyone in getting withdrawn children to talk to me — I would fix Ted straight in the eye and carried on normal conversation."

HELEN THOMSON

"Staffordshire Education Authority turned a Teddy into an aid to help deaf children learn to vary pitch and pronounce syllables. His eyes fade or brighten according to pitch and volume and one little girl who could make no sound at all responded within five minutes to Fred's gadgetry."

PETER BULL
from "Book of Teddy Bears"

"Parents and others are very arbitrary in deciding when a child should stop having his or her Teddy bear around. My mother thought sixteen was about the right time. I still think she was wrong and I'm sure Theodore agrees with me."

PETER BULL

"It's hard to visualize the toys you had fifty years ago — all save bear. He's as clear as if he were sitting on the desk in front of you. . . . of course . . . he probably *is.*"

PAM BROWN

"Over the years my sons had somehow managed to adopt fifty-five teds. At twelve years of age they *had* to hide them from friends who came to stay. But now — both sons over twenty — special teds are allowed to come out when gran visits or someone is ill. And, one or two lucky teddies have got a lovely new lady help care for them."

HELEN   EXLEY

"To a child, Teddy is a bridge between a human and an animal. He doesn't mind being taken for a walk, dressed in ridiculous hats, or even being read to. You can blame him for anything, and he won't deny it. His marvellous face expresses anything a child wants to feel or hear."

PETER BULL

"A bear knows all your secrets — and keeps schtum."

ROSANNE AMBROSE-BROWN

"There's just something about a Teddy bear that's impossible to explain. When you hold one in your arms, you get a feeling of love, comfort and security.
It's almost supernatural"

JAMES OWNBY

"In a notorious 'sex and bribes' trial, a Mr Maurice Cochrane, the Managing Director of a big company under investigation, was reported as having 'sat cuddling a huge Teddy Bear to which he occasionally referred for advice, when he interviewed three prospective salesmen.'"

PETER BULL
from "Book of Teddy Bears"

"I didn't know if my husband would understand about my Teddy bear, who's been sharing my bed since I was four. But they had a long talk, and my husband discovered some things about Teddy that even I didn't know — like some nights Teddy would rather watch TV all night in the living room."

LAURIE DILSON

"My son is getting married in Australia next week. His fiancée has installed a large cloth poodle in their new home. He has agreed. As long as we can air mail 'Father Bear' in time for the wedding."

CLARA ORTEGA

"Love me, love my teddy bear."

SAMANTHA ARMSTRONG

"They've even coined a name for teddy lovers in general, it's Arctophile (from the Greek 'arkos', meaning bear and 'philos', meaning friends)."

LEO ZANELLI

"My son made me promise to keep all thirty-eight of his teds forever — no matter where he went."

HELEN EXLEY

"Collectors are now springing up all over the world. In America, Mrs Patricia Fitt has a "teddy bear workshop" consisting of seventy-four little Sieff teddy bears: while in Britain, Miss Sheila Coull has a teddy collection of 215 — a number beaten by Mrs Audrey Duck with over 240!"

LEO ZANELLI

Pooh's Birthday Hum 1979

I'm not so young and nifty
On the fourteenth I'll be fifty
So my friends must not be thrifty
On the day

My skin's a little tighter and
My hair is slightly whiter
But I'm sprighter and I'm brighter
Than a jay

I've got a little lumpy
And I'm not so up-and-jumpy
But I'm still quite nice and dumpy
In the tum

My nose is not so furry
And my eyes are rather blurry
But my voice is always purry
When I hum

Though the cars are fast and grumbly
And the towns are long and rumbly
I live in my own bumbly
Kind of way

A. A. MILNE
WILLA-JANE ADDIS

— ◆ —

"A washed bear is not a happy bear."

PAM BROWN

"Baths may be lovely for people — adult
people that is, but bears are not that keen.
When did you last see or hear of a bear taking
a bath, willingly?"

TED MENTON
from "The Teddy Bear Lovers Catalogue"

"There are few sadder sights than a wet bear
hanging from the washing line by
its ears. It says a lot for them that they
never complain."

PAM BROWN

"Where is he now? I don't know. He got lost in the shuffle of what is called the growing-up process, but he never stopped following me, and sometimes when I thoughtfully look back, there he is looking at me with that surprised expression that says, 'Hi! How y' doing?'"

MARCUS BACH

"The teddy bear is the last toy we part with. He is all that is left of that lost world where solutions seemed possible and a friend who saw no fault and made no reproach, waited forever in the old armchair."

PAM BROWN

"A teddy bear is your childhood wrapped up
in faded yellow fur, and as such,
he commands affection long after
he is outgrown."

PAM BROWN

— ◆ —

Safe were those evenings of the
pre-war world
When firelight shone on green linoleum;
I heard the church bells hollowing out
the sky,
Deep beyond deep, like never-ending stars,
And turned to Archibald, my safe old bear,
Whose woollen eyes looked sad or glad
at me,
Whose ample forehead I could wet
with tears,
Whose half-moon ears received my confidence,
Who made me laugh, who never let
me down.
I used to wait for hours to see him move,
Convinced that he could breathe.
One dreadful day
They hid him from me as a punishment:
Sometimes the desolation of that loss
Comes back to me and I must go upstairs
To see him in the sawdust, so to speak,
Safe and returned to his idolater.

JOHN BETJEMAN
from "Summoned by Bells"

"I was pushing my cart down the grocery store aisle, mind focused on bananas and boxed cereal, when I was distracted by a shelf of Teddy bears. One seemed to be reaching out to me. I checked my shopping list, but there were no 'Bears' written down. I try to avoid impulse buying, and started on down the aisle. I guess I needed that bear, because I wheeled my cart around, and in he went, sitting happily on a head of lettuce."

MOLLY COURVILLE

"Now that I'm all grown up, I can buy any old Teddy bear I want —
except the old Teddy Bear I want."

WILLIAM STERNMAN

"A row of Teddy bears sitting in a toyshop, all one size, all one price. Yet how different each is from the next. Some look gay, some look sad. Some look standoffish, some look lovable. And one in particular, that one over there, has a specially endearing expression. Yes, that is the one we would like, please."

CHRISTOPHER MILNE
from "The Enchanted Places"

TEDDY BEAR

A bear, however hard he tries,
Grows tubby without exercise.
Our Teddy Bear is short and fat,
Which is not to be wondered at;
He gets what exercise he can
By falling off the ottoman,
But generally seems to lack
The energy to clamber back.

Now tubbiness is just the thing
Which gets a fellow wondering;
And Teddy worried lots about
The fact that he was rather stout.
He thought: "If only I were thin!
But how does anyone begin?"
He thought: "It really isn't fair
To grudge me exercise and air.

A. A. MILNE

"Going on a journey with children means checking; Two bags, one umbrella, one pushchair, two children, two bears. Purse, ticket. Recheck bears."

PAM BROWN

"Why do I leave the zip of my bag a little open? So that the bear can breathe, of course."

PATRICIA HITCHCOCK

"What is it about this inanimate object of fur and stuffing that makes it so hard to part with? As children, we were acutely aware of just how much our bears loved us, and we filled their ears with our daily doings and deepest confidences. How could one grow up and not take along this dearest of companions?"

SARAH McCLENNAN

"The basic ingredient in any leaving-home case is the bear."

JOHNNIE HAGUE

"One day, when I was all grown up and sad,
I happened to meet Teddy in the attic.
Suddenly the years dropped away, and I felt
young and loved again."

HELEN FREISER

— ◆ —

"Every child has his Pooh, but one would think it odd if every man still kept his Pooh to remind him of his childhood. But my Pooh is different, you say. He is *the* Pooh. No, this only makes him different to you, not different to me. My toys were and are to me no more than yours were and are to you."

CHRISTOPHER MILNE
from "The Enchanted Places"

"Meet one's teddy in the attic after several years and find yourself overwhelmed with concern. He looks so *ill*.
So bring him down and brush what little hair he has left. And sit him in the armchair by the fire."

JESSE O'NEILL

"Teddy bears accompanied RAF pilots into air dogfights and the Battle of Britain and GIs to Vietnam."

PAM HOBBS
from "Collecting Teddy Bears"

"Junior officers in Napoleon's army carried a Field Marshall's baton in their haversacks. Junior officers in the British Army are more likely to carry a teddy bear. They <u>say</u> it's a lucky mascot."

JENNY DE VRIES

"Remember when I said Teddy can't sleep without me? Well, truth is, I can't sleep without Teddy."

WEBSTER PAPADOPOLIS

"An experienced Teddy Bear brings with him a lifetime of knowledge and experience; the wisdom of silence and stillness in moments of great turmoil. The long-suffering patience that is learned when belonging to a child who is coming of age, and coping with the bewilderment that this period of time can bring, is what he does best. The experienced bear has seen life through the heart and eyes of a child grown to adulthood and perhaps even accompanied that adult all the way to the end of the road."

TED MENTON
from "The Teddy Bear Lovers Catalogue"

"How did children ever manage
before bears?"

JESSE O'NEILL

"Henry Middleditch, an Insurance Broker,
sued his former wife for the return of an
eighteenth century table, a cut glass decanter
and his Teddy Bear."

PETER BULL
from "Bear With Me"

"My son broke his collar bone. When I had
to leave for work, he asked if Teddy could
also have his shoulder bandaged up.
I carefully did it, giving Teddy plenty of love
and cuddles and a big kiss. I waved goodbye
to two happy invalids."

HELEN EXLEY

"You need a bear
to get you through measles.
Especially when you're
supposed to have grown up."

CLARA ORTEGA

— ◆ —

"All you have between you
and 'The Dark' is Bear."

HELEN THOMSON

— ◆ —

*F*URRY BEAR

If I were a bear,
And a big bear too,
I shouldn't much care
If it froze or snew;
I shouldn't much mind
If it snowed or friz —
I'd be all fur-lined
With a coat like his!

For I'd have fur boots and a brown fur wrap,
And brown fur knickers and a brown fur cap.
I'd have a fur muffle-ruff to cover my jaws,
And brown fur mittens on my big brown paws.
With a big brown furry-down up to my head,
I'd sleep all the winter in a big fur bed.

A. A. MILNE

"The Teddy Bear has come to stay, so perfectly is his grizzly exterior adapted to fitting into the many chubby arms which are extended to him. He is not only bear-like enough to lift him above juvenile criticism but he is possessed of those semi-human attributes which fit him eminently for youthful companionship. He is every inch a bear and yet he certainly embodies exactly the doll qualities which are demanded by the child of today. He is well-made and set up. His head really turns round and his legs are nicely adjustable. He has, moreover, the precious gift of true adaptability; he can be made to crawl, climb, stand or sit and in each pose he is not only delightfully himself, but he also suggests to the imaginative owner whatever special being his fancy would have his teddy personify."

CAROLINE TICKNER
from "New England Magazine"

"The teddy bear plays a great part in the psychological development of people of all ages over the world. This is because he is a truly international figure that is non-religious and yet is universally recognized as a symbol of love and affection.

He represents friendship. He functions as a leavening influence amid the trials and tribulations of life."

COLONEL BOB (ROBERT) HENDERSON
from "Bear Tracks"

— ◆ —

"In a world where everyone seems to be larger
and louder than yourself, it is very comforting
to have a small, quiet companion."

PETER GRAY

"When everyone else has let you down,
there's always Ted."

CLARA ORTEGA

ACKNOWLEDGEMENTS

The publishers gratefully acknowledge permission to reproduce copyright material in this book. While every effort has been made to trace copyright holders, the publishers would like to hear from any not here acknowledged.

Sir John Betjeman: extract from *Summoned by Bells*. Reprinted by permission of John Murray (Publishers) Ltd.

Ted Menton: extracts from *The Teddy Bear Lovers Catalogue*. Reprinted by permission of Ebury Press, London.

"Furry Bear", from *Now we are Six* by A.A. Milne illustrations by E.H. Shepard. Copyright 1927 by E.P. Dutton, renewed © 1955 by A.A. Milne. Used by permission of Dutton Children's Books, a division of Penguin Books USA Inc. and Methuen Children's Books, a division of Reed Consumer Books Ltd.

"Teddy Bear", from *When we were very Young* by A.A. Milne illustrations by E.H. Shepard. Copyright 1924 by E.P Dutton, renewed 1952 by A.A. Milne. Used by permission of Dutton Children's Books, a division of Penguin Books USA Inc. and Methuen Children's Books, a division of Reed Consumer Books Ltd.

Extract from *Winnie-the-Pooh* by A.A. Milne, illustrations by E.H. Shepard. Copyright 1926 by E.P. Dutton, renewed 1954 by A.A. Milne. Used by permission of Dutton Children's Books, a division of Reed Consumer Books Ltd.

Christopher Milne: extracts from *The Enchanted Places*. Reprinted by permission of Methuen, London and Curtis Brown Ltd, London.

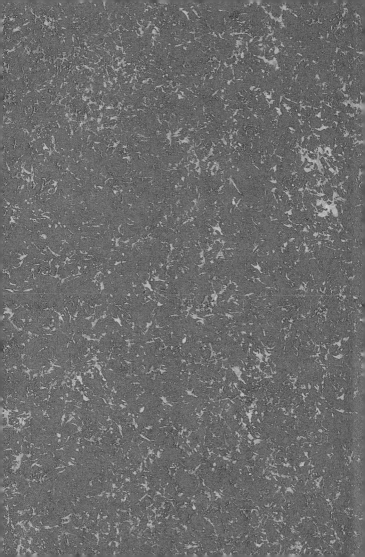